SCHIRMER'S LIBRARY
OF MUSICAL CLASSICS

Vol. 2121

THE ROMANTIC ERA
PIANO ALBUM

51 Favorite Pieces by

Brahms	Mendelssohn
Chopin	Rachmaninoff
Fauré	Schubert
Field	Schumann
Grieg	Scriabin
Liszt	Tchaikovsky

ISBN 978-1-4950-5164-7

G. SCHIRMER, Inc.

DISTRIBUTED BY

7777 W. BLUEMOUND RD. P.O. BOX 13819 MILWAUKEE, WI 53213

Copyright © 2016 by G. Schirmer, Inc. (ASCAP) New York, NY
International Copyright Secured. All Rights Reserved.
Warning: Unauthorized reproduction of this publication is
prohibited by Federal law and subject to criminal prosecution.

www.musicsalesclassical.com
www.halleonard.com

CONTENTS

CONTENTS

INTERMEZZO
in A-flat Major

Johannes Brahms
Op. 76, No. 3

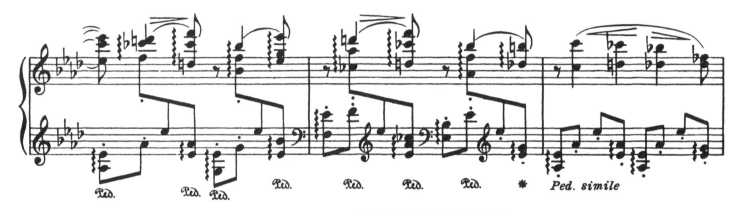

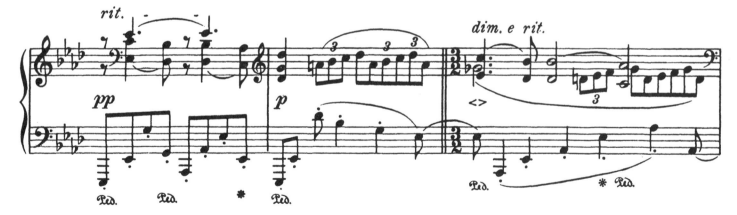

INTERMEZZO
in B-flat Major

Johannes Brahms
Op. 76, No. 4

Allegretto grazioso

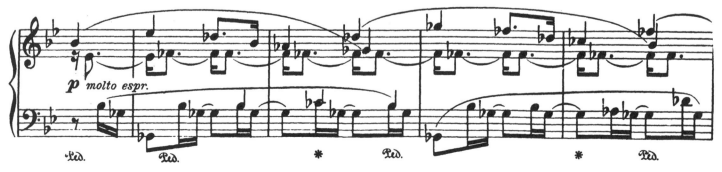

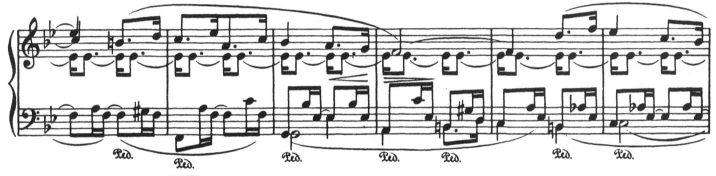

INTERMEZZO
in A Major

Johannes Brahms
Op. 76, No. 6

Andante con moto
Sanft bewegt

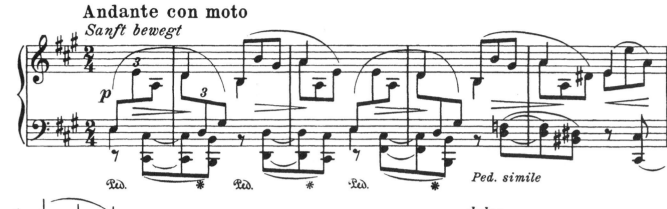

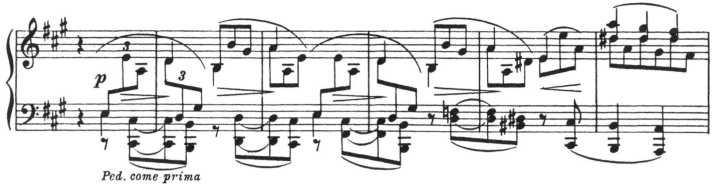

CAPRICCIO
in B minor

Johannes Brahms
Op. 76, No. 2

Allegretto non troppo

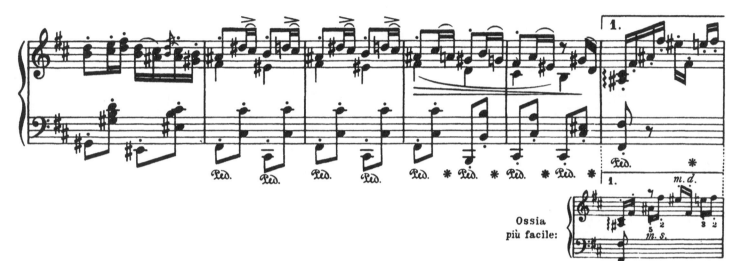

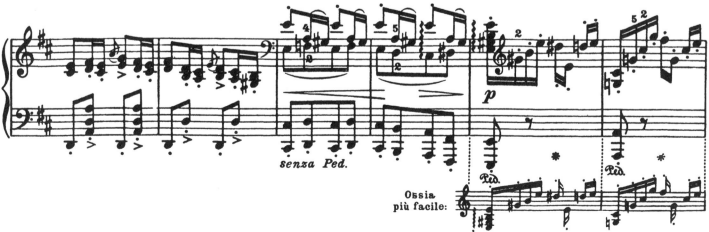

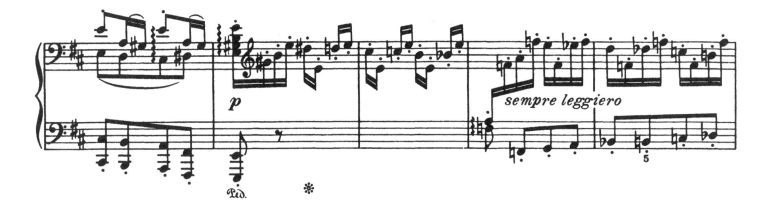

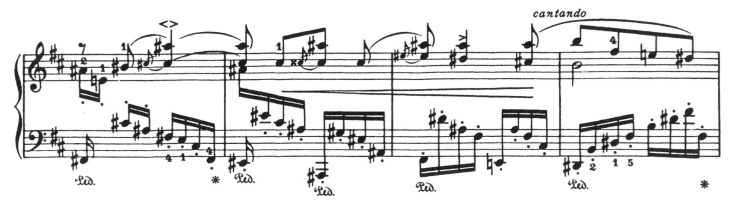

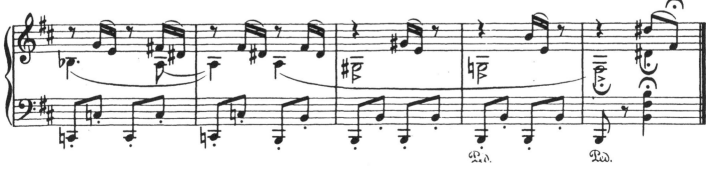

RHAPSODY
in G minor

Johannes Brahms
Op. 79, No. 2

Molto passionato, ma non troppo allegro

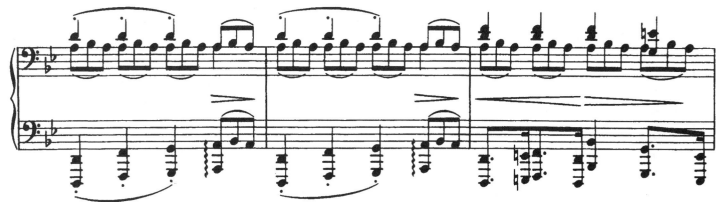

INTERMEZZO
in A Major

Johannes Brahms
Op. 118, No. 2

Andante teneramente

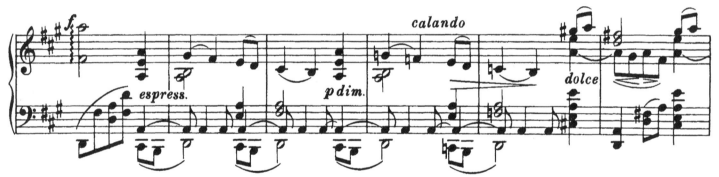

CAPRICCIO

in G minor

Johannes Brahms
Op. 116, No. 3

Allegro passionato

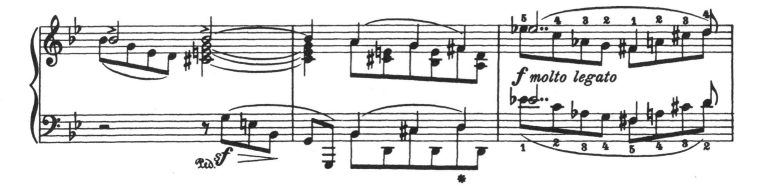

Un poco meno Allegro

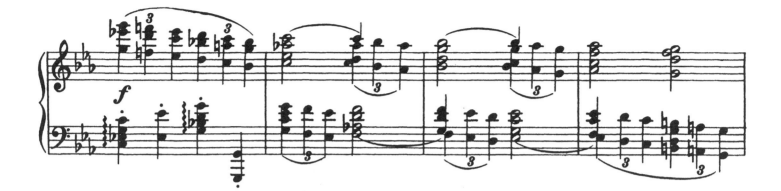

Tempo I.

à F. Liszt

ÉTUDE
in E Major

Frédéric Chopin
Op. 10, No. 3

Lento ma non troppo (♩ = 69)

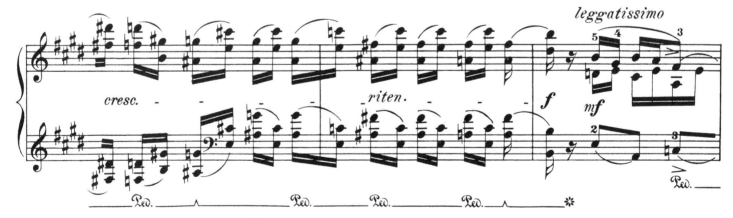

à F. Liszt

ÉTUDE
in C minor

Frédéric Chopin
Op. 10, No. 12

Allegro con fuoco (♩ = 144)

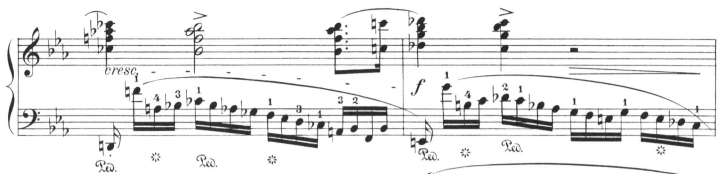

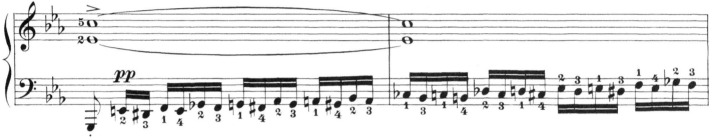

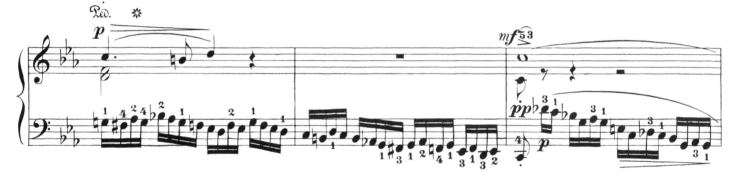

FANTAISIE-IMPROMPTU
in C-sharp minor

Frédéric Chopin
Op. 66 (Posthumous)

Allegro agitato

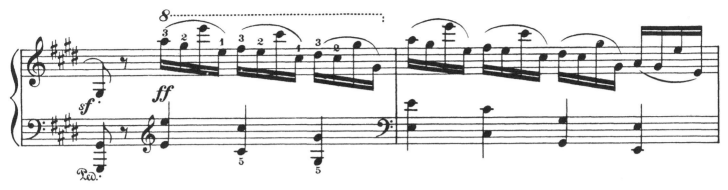

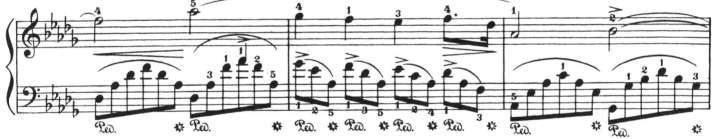

Tempo I° (Allegro agitato)

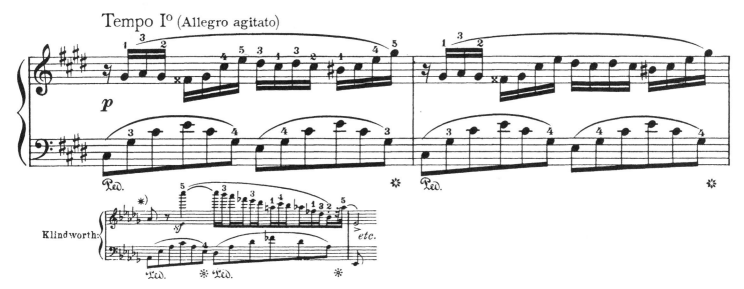

Klindworth:

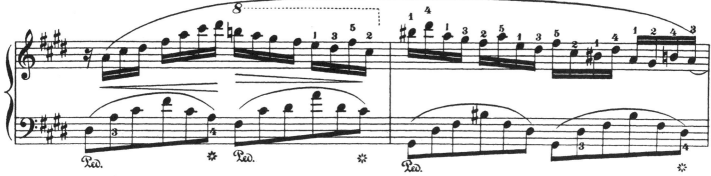

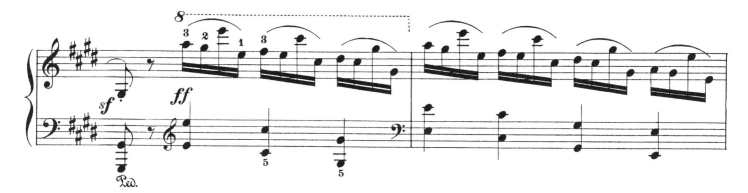

à Mademoiselle Lina Freppa

MAZURKA
in B-flat Major

Frédéric Chopin
Op. 17, No. 1

Vivo e risoluto (♩ = 160)

D. C. al Fine

à Mademoiselle Lina Freppa

MAZURKA

in E minor

Frédéric Chopin
Op. 17, No. 2

Lento, ma non troppo (♩ = 144)

à Mademoiselle Lina Freppa

MAZURKA
in A minor

Frédéric Chopin
Op. 17, No. 4

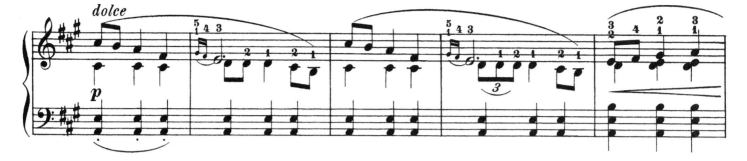

à Madame Camilla Pleyel

NOCTURNE
in E-flat Major

Frédéric Chopin
Op. 9, No. 2

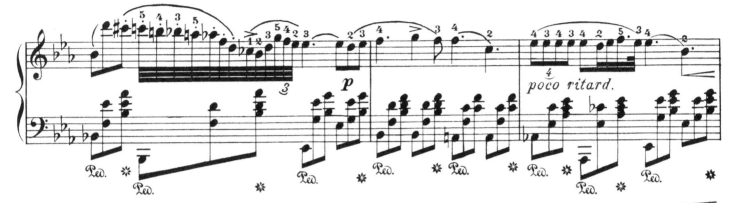

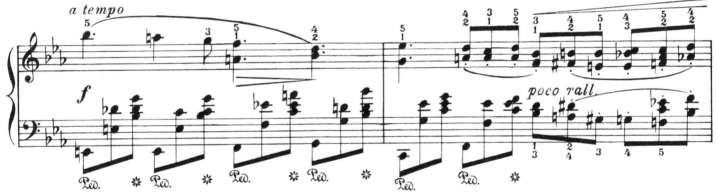

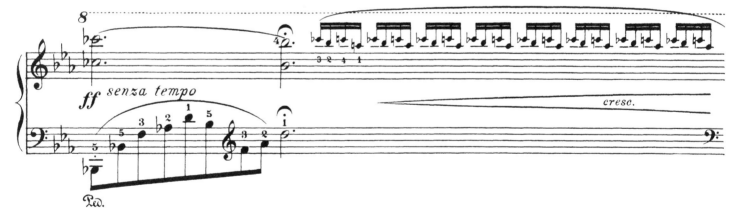

à J. C. Kessler

PRÉLUDE
in E minor

Frédéric Chopin
Op. 28, No. 4

à Mademoiselle Laura Duperré

NOCTURNE
in C minor

Frédéric Chopin
Op. 48, No. 1

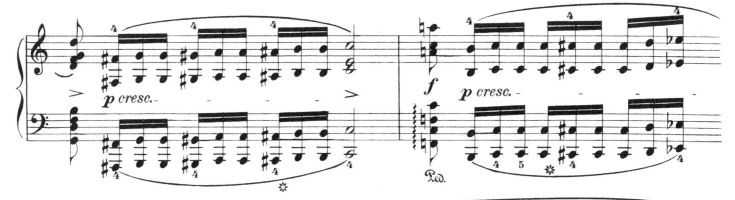

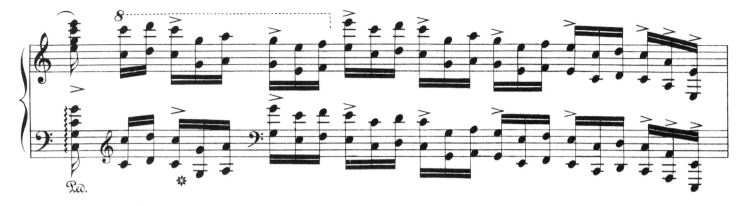

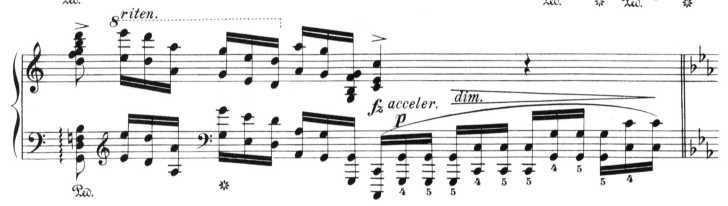

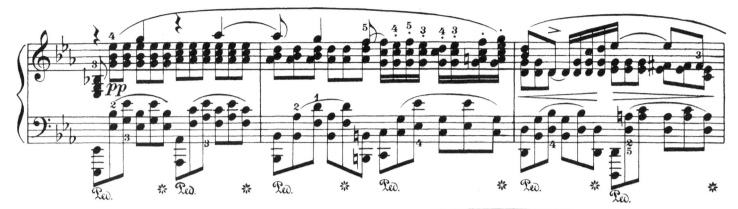

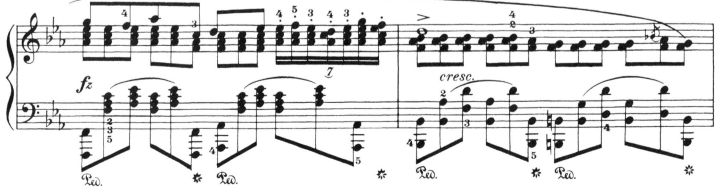

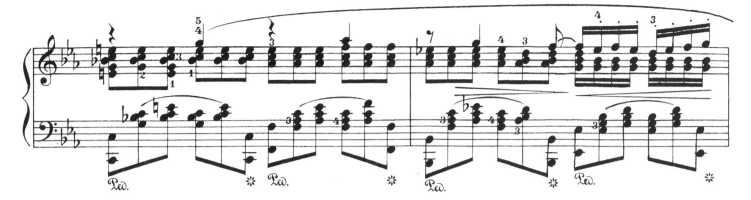

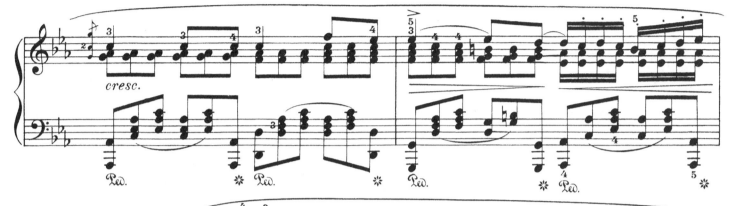

à *J. C. Kessler*

PRÉLUDE
in F-sharp Major

Frédéric Chopin
Op. 28, No. 13

à J. C. Kessler

PRÉLUDE
in A-flat Major

Frédéric Chopin
Op. 28, No. 17

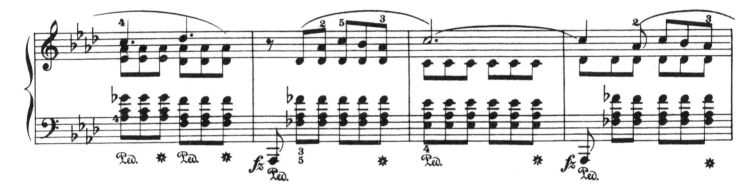

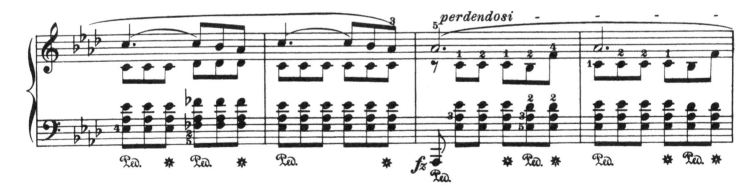

à Madame la Comtesse Delphine Potocka

WALTZ
in D-flat Major

Frédéric Chopin
Op. 64, No. 1

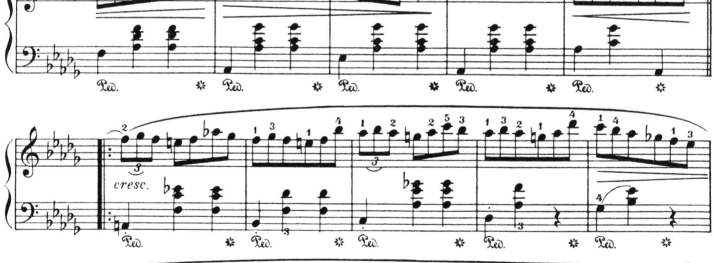

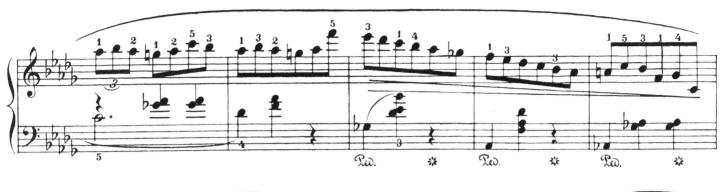

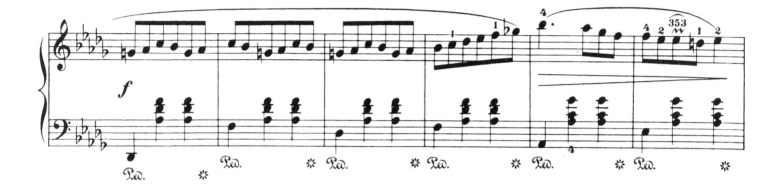

WALTZ
in A minor

Frédéric Chopin
KK. IVb, No. 11

Allegretto

à J. C. Kessler

PRÉLUDE
in D-flat Major

Frédéric Chopin
Op. 28, No. 15

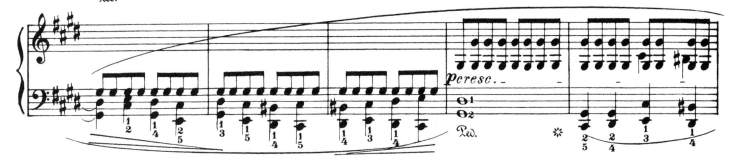

BERCEUSE
in E Major

Gabriel Fauré
Op. 56, No. 1

NOCTURNE
in E minor

John Field

HOME SICKNESS

from *Lyric Pieces*

Edvard Grieg
Op. 57, No. 6

Molto più vivo

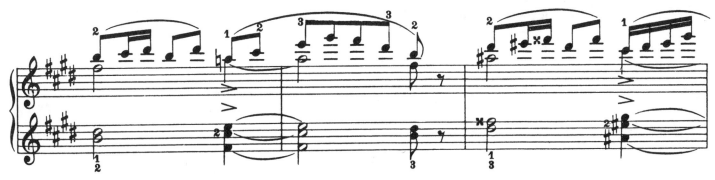

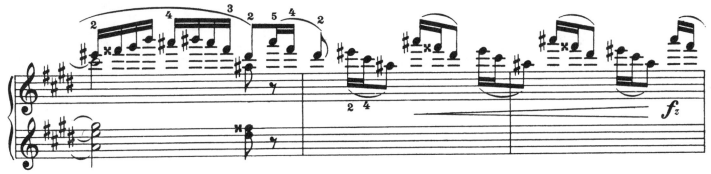

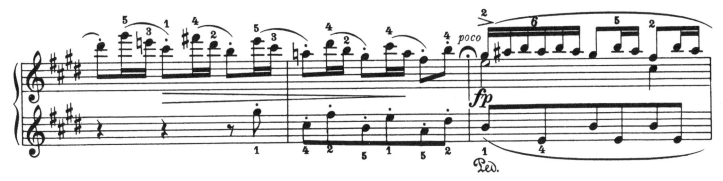

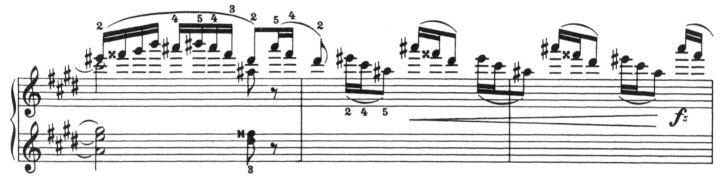

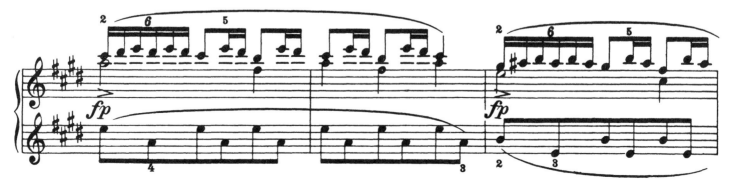

Tempo I

poco a poco più lento al Fine

WEDDING DAY AT TROLDHAUGEN

from *Lyric Pieces*

Edvard Grieg
Op. 65, No. 6

Tempo di Marcia un poco vivace

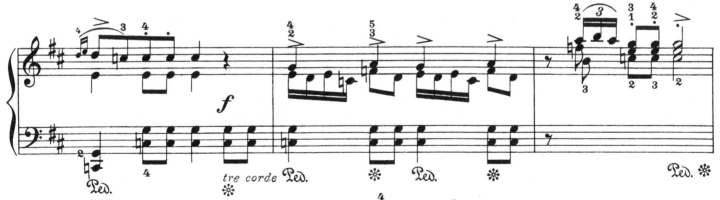

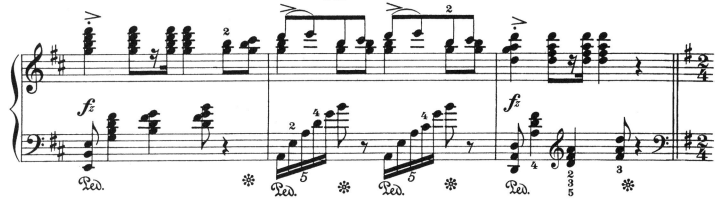

98

Tempo I

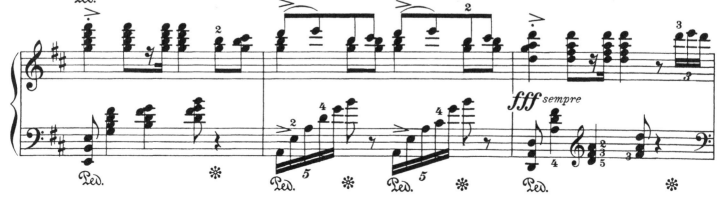

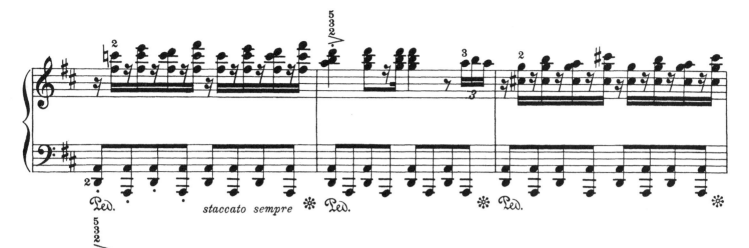

LIEBESTRAUM NO. 3

from *Liebesträume*

Franz Liszt

Poco allegro, con affetto

dolce cantando

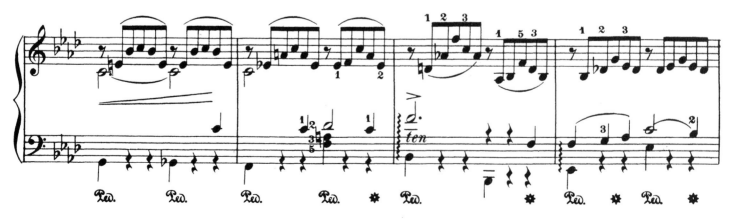

poco cresc. ed agitato

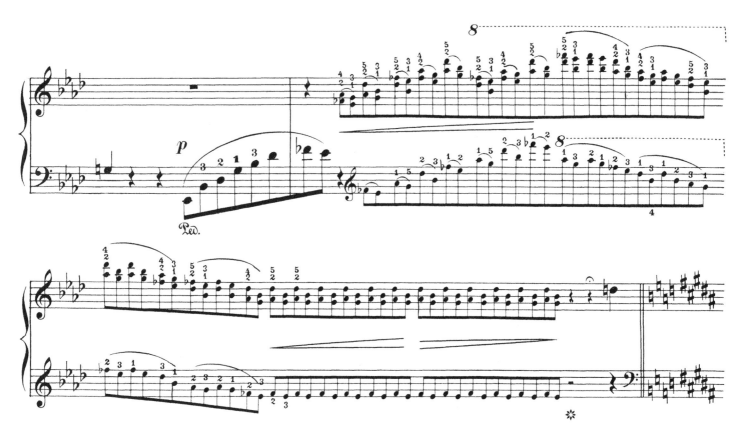

Più animato, con passione

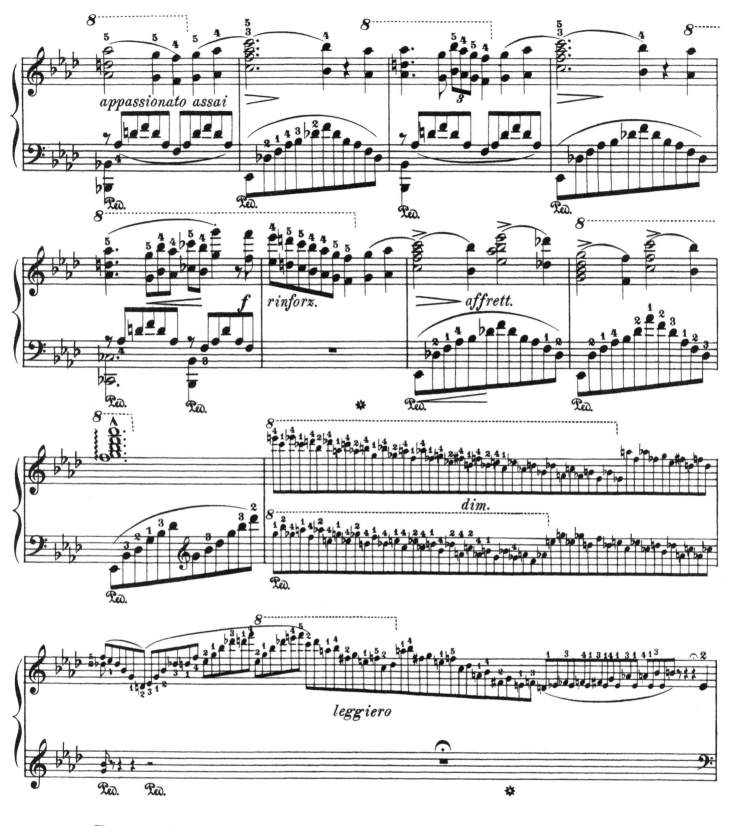

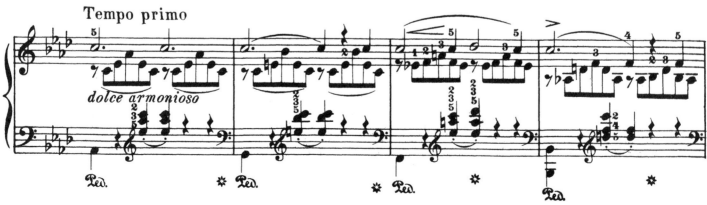

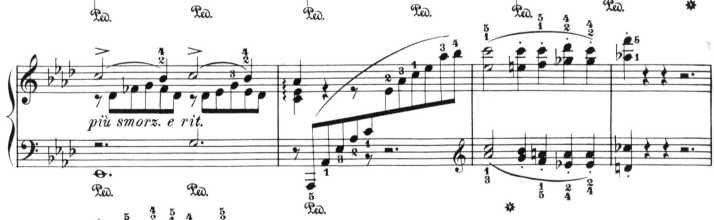

MEDITATION
from *Songs Without Words*

Felix Mendelssohn
Op. 67, No. 1

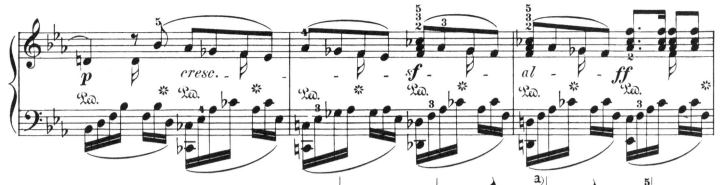

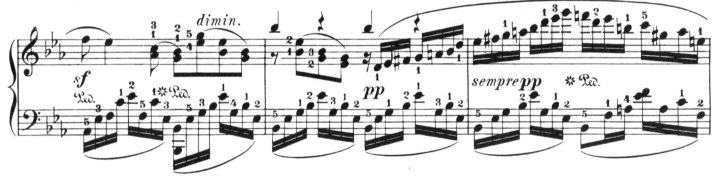

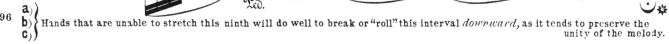

25496

a)
b) Hands that are unable to stretch this ninth will do well to break or "roll" this interval *downward*, as it tends to preserve the
c) unity of the melody.

VENETIAN BOAT SONG NO. 2

from *Songs Without Words*

Felix Mendelssohn
Op. 30, No. 6

Allegretto tranquillo

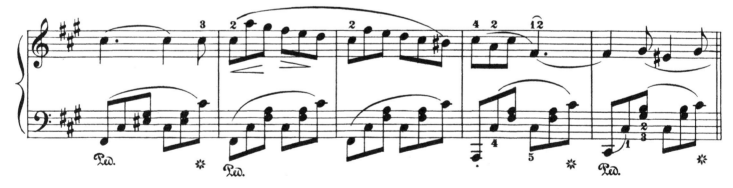

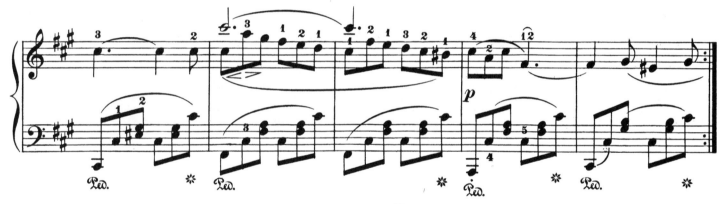

PRÉLUDE
in D Major

Sergei Rachmaninoff
Op. 23, No. 4

Copyright © 1994 by G. Schirmer, Inc., (ASCAP) New York, NY
International Copyright Secured. All Rights Reserved.
Warning: Unauthorized reproduction of this publication is
prohibited by Federal law and subject to criminal prosecution.

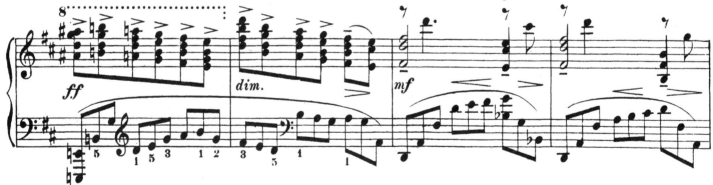

PRÉLUDE
in G minor

Sergei Rachmaninoff
Op. 23, No. 5

Alla marcia (♩=108)

Copyright © 1994 by G. Schirmer, Inc., (ASCAP) New York, NY
International Copyright Secured. All Rights Reserved.
Warning: Unauthorized reproduction of this publication is
prohibited by Federal law and subject to criminal prosecution.

Un poco meno mosso

poco a poco accelerando e cresc. al Tempo I

Tempo I

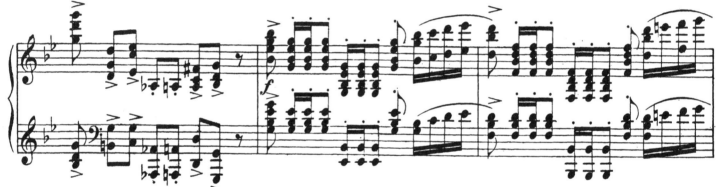

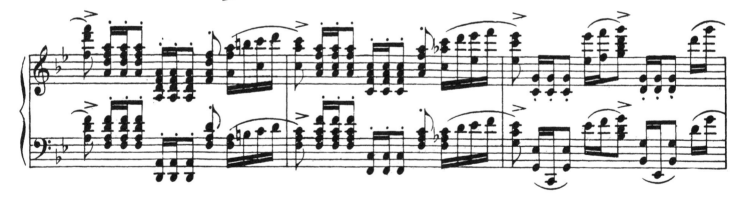

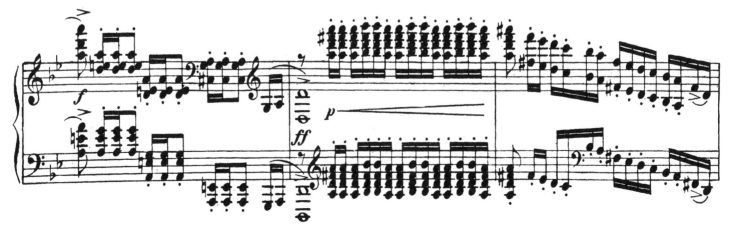

PRÉLUDE
in B minor

Sergei Rachmaninoff
Op. 32, No. 10

Copyright © 1911 (Renewed) by Hawkes & Son (London) Limited
International Copyright Secured. All Rights Reserved.
Warning: Unauthorized reproduction of this publication is
prohibited by Federal law and subject to criminal prosecution.

126

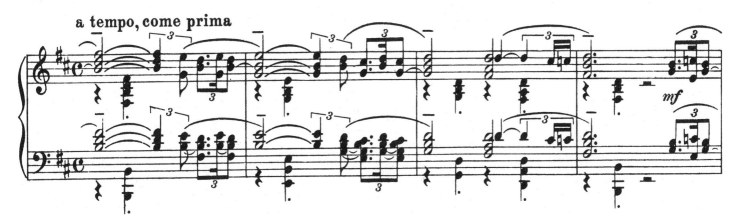

PRÉLUDE
in C-sharp minor

(**Andante**)

Sergei Rachmaninoff
Op. 3, No. 2

Copyright © 1898, 1925 (Renewed) by G. Schirmer, Inc., (ASCAP) New York, NY
International Copyright Secured. All Rights Reserved.
**Warning: Unauthorized reproduction of this publication is
prohibited by Federal law and subject to criminal prosecution.**

Agitato

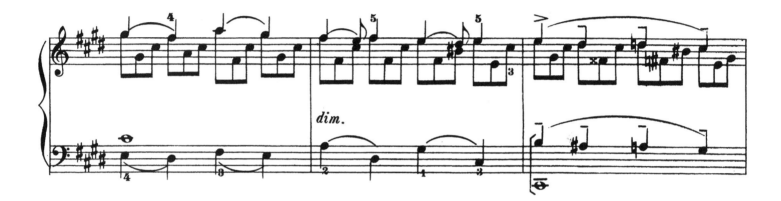

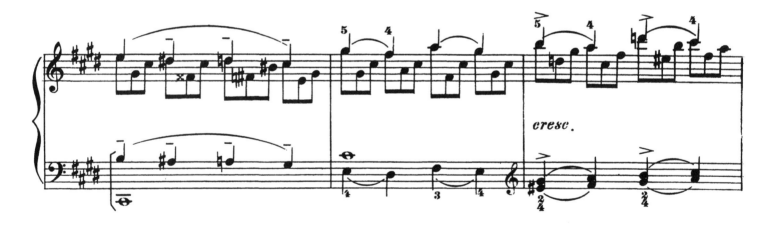

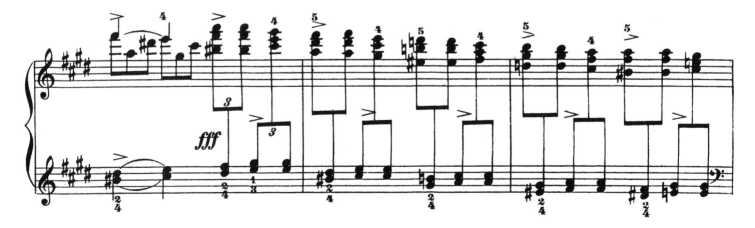

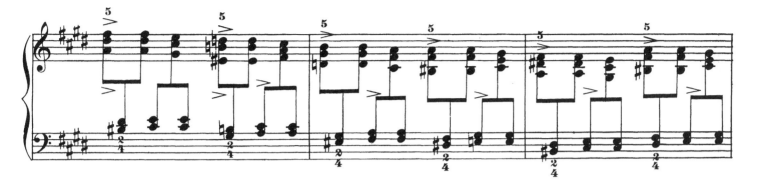

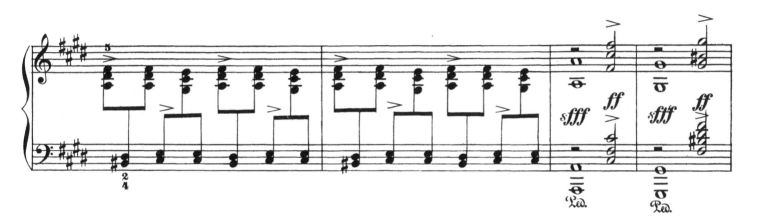

Tempo I

WARUM? (WHY?)

from *Fantasiestücke*

Robert Schumann
Op. 12, No. 3

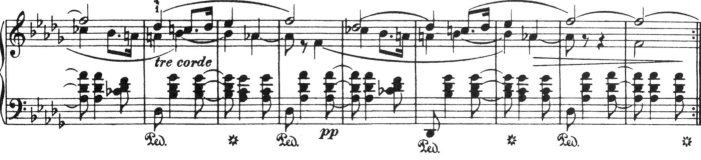

ABOUT STRANGE LANDS AND PEOPLE

Von fremden Ländern und Menschen

from *Scenes from Childhood (Kinderszenen)*

Robert Schumann
Op. 15, No. 1

Copyright © 1945 by G. Schirmer, Inc. (ASCAP) New York, NY
International Copyright Secured. All Rights Reserved.
**Warning: Unauthorized reproduction of this publication is
prohibited by Federal law and subject to criminal prosecution.**

PLEADING CHILD

Bittendes Kind

from *Scenes from Childhood (Kinderszenen)*

Robert Schumann
Op. 15, No. 4

PERFECTLY CONTENTED

Glückes genug

from *Scenes from Childhood (Kinderszenen)*

Robert Schumann
Op. 15, No. 5

REVERIE
Träumerei
from *Scenes from Childhood (Kinderszenen)*

Robert Schumann
Op. 15, No. 7

AT THE FIRESIDE

Am Kamin

from *Scenes from Childhood (Kinderszenen)*

Robert Schumann
Op. 15, No. 8

PRÉLUDE
in E minor

Alexander Scriabin
Op. 11, No. 4

PRÉLUDE
in A-flat Major

Alexander Scriabin
Op. 11, No. 17

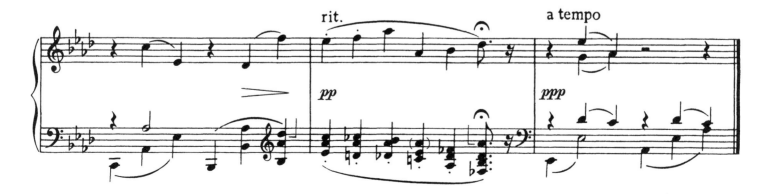

PRÉLUDE
in G minor

Alexander Scriabin
Op. 11, No. 22

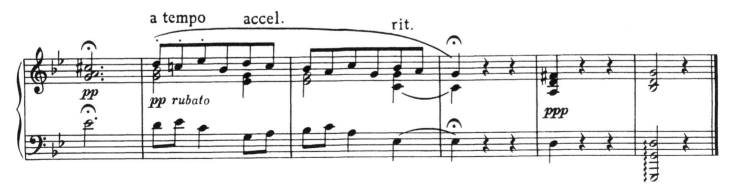

1) Scriabin often played the last chord in this measure *f*, followed by an immediate *pp* in the following bar, yielding an echo effect.

PRÉLUDE

for the Left Hand
in C-sharp minor

Alexander Scriabin
Op. 9, No. 1

Andante

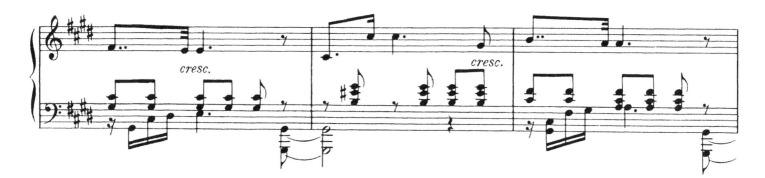

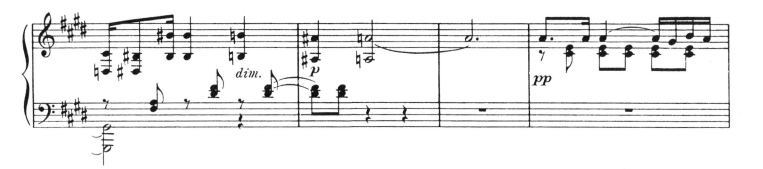

PRÉLUDE

in G-sharp minor

Alexander Scriabin
Op. 22, No. 1

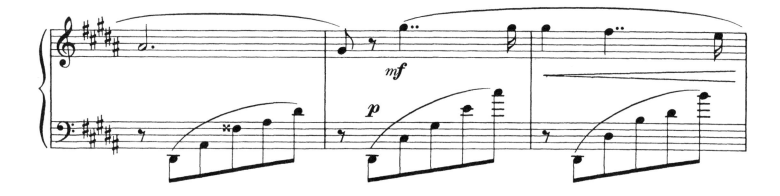

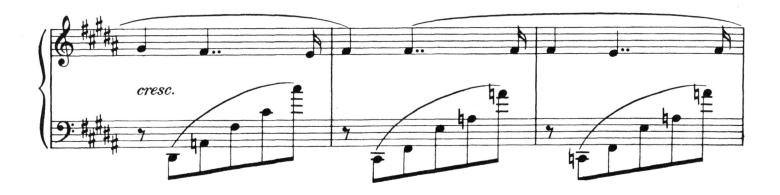

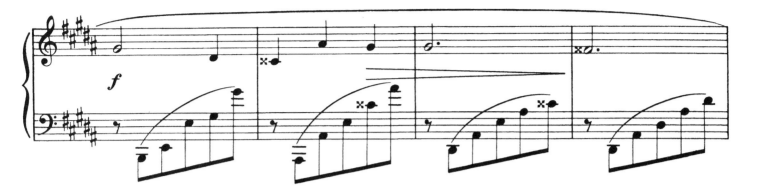

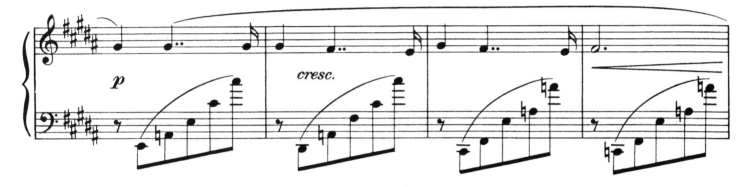

IMPROMPTU
in G-flat Major

Franz Schubert
Op. 90, No. 3

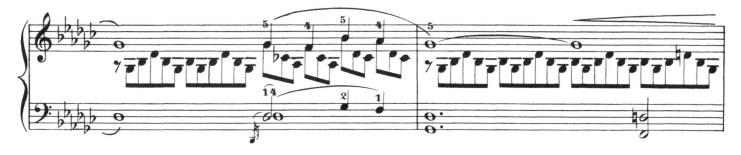

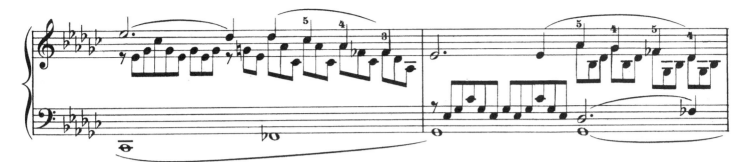

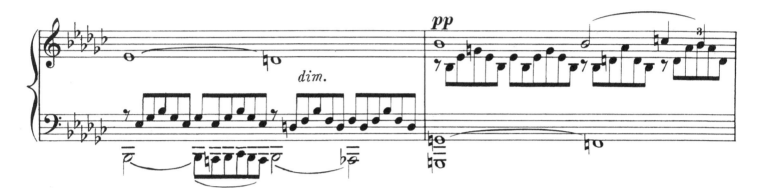

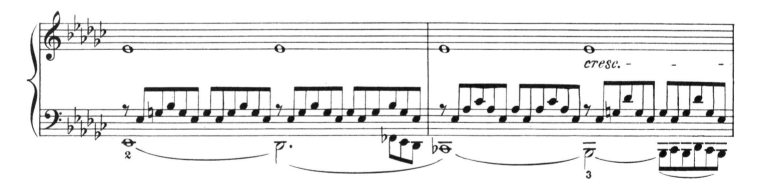

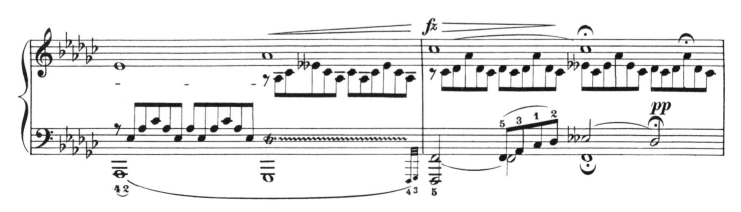

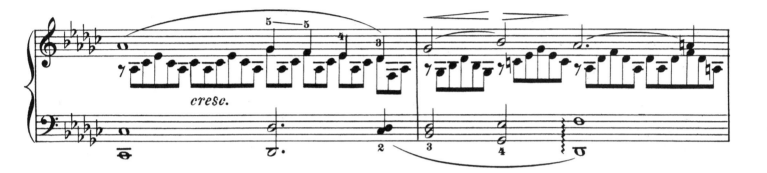

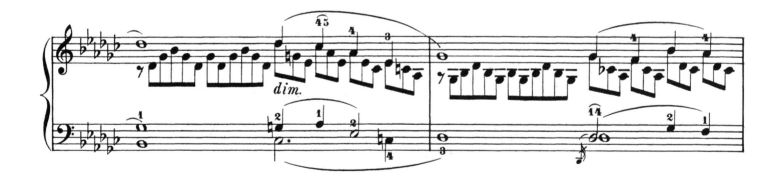

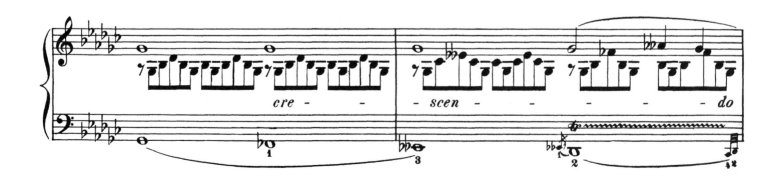

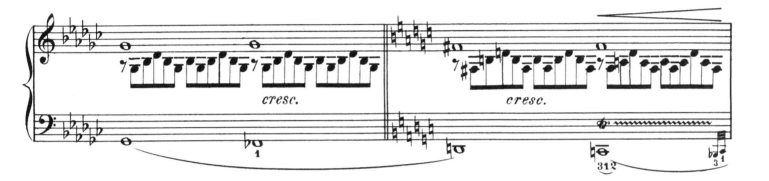

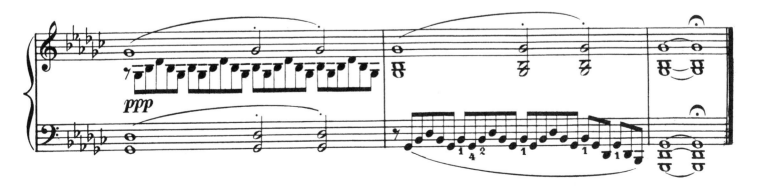

MOMENT MUSICAL
in A-flat Major

Franz Schubert
Op. 94, No. 2

Andante (♩. = 72)

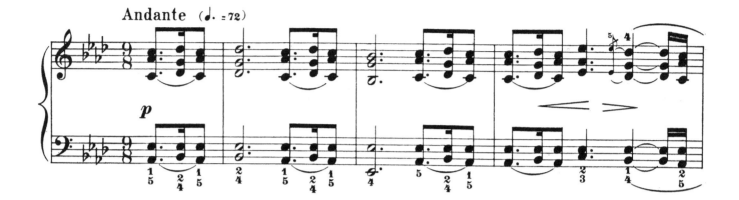

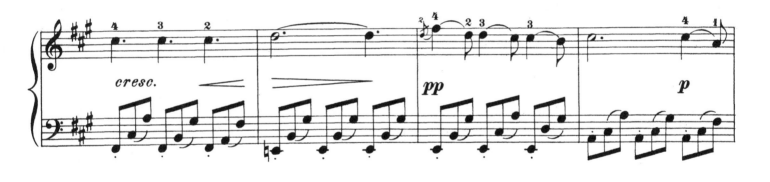

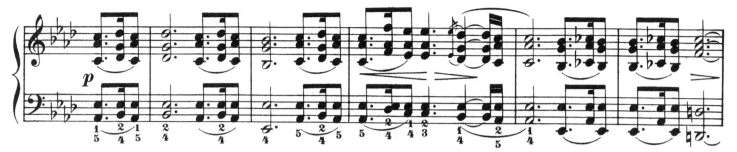

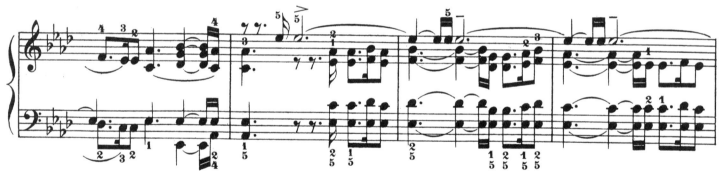

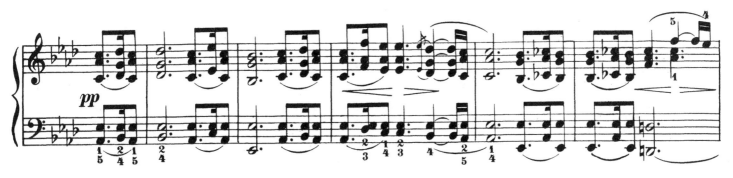

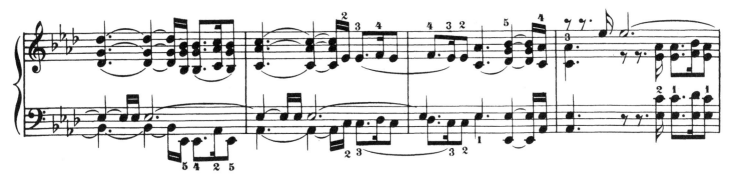

MOMENT MUSICAL

in F minor

Franz Schubert
Op. 94, No. 3

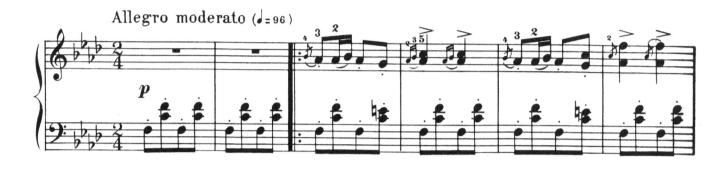

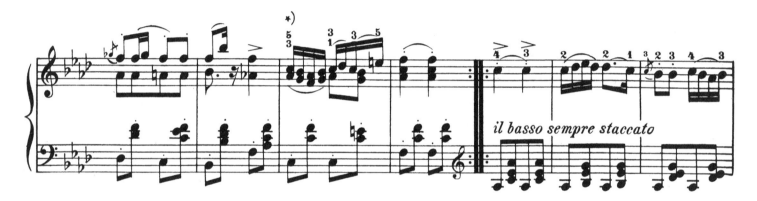

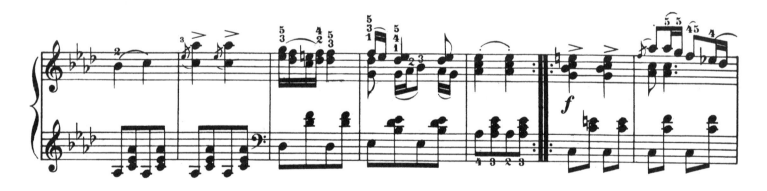

*) May also be
played thus:

IMPROMPTU
in A-flat Major

Franz Schubert
Op. 142, No. 2

Allegretto (♩ = 132)

Trio

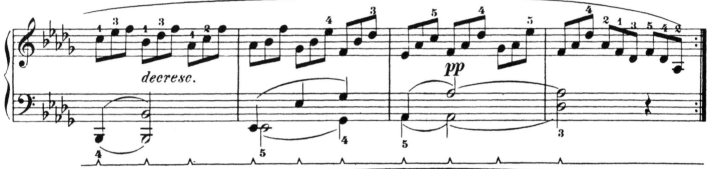

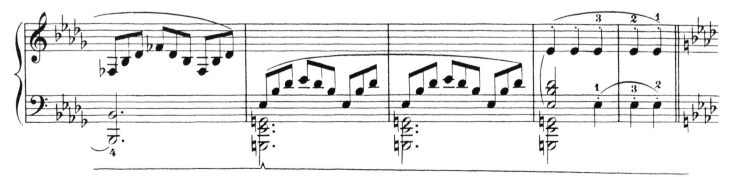

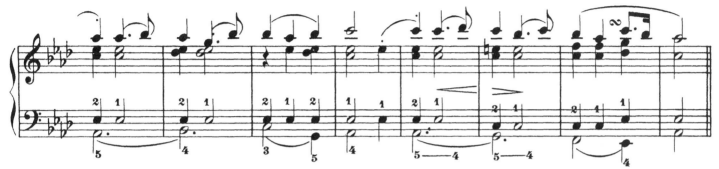

SWEET DREAMS

from *Album for the Young*

Pyotr Il'yich Tchaikovsky
Op. 39, No. 21

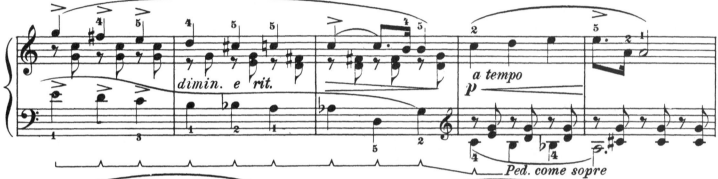

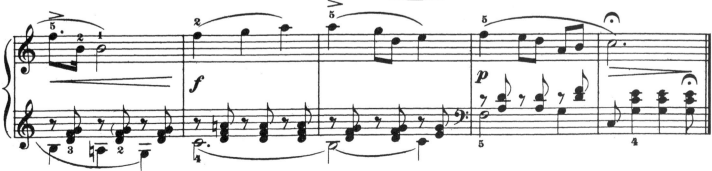

JUNE

from *The Seasons*

Pyotr Il'yich Tchaikovsky
Op. 37b, No. 6

Andante cantabile.

NOVEMBER

Troika

from *The Seasons*

Pyotr Il'yich Tchaikovsky
Op. 37b, No. 11

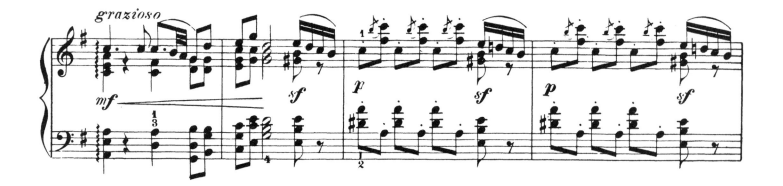

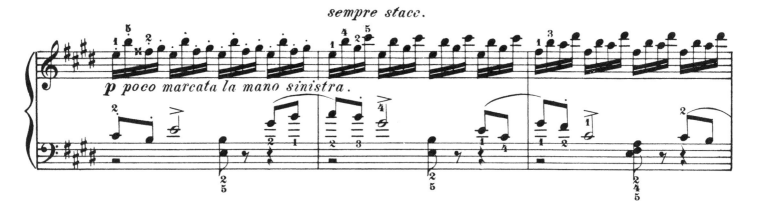

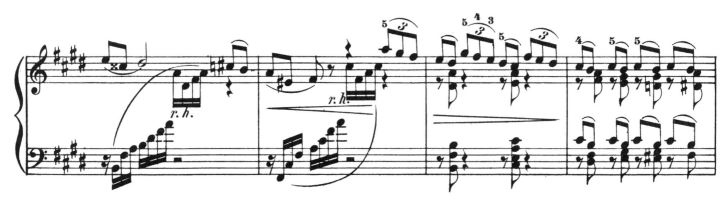

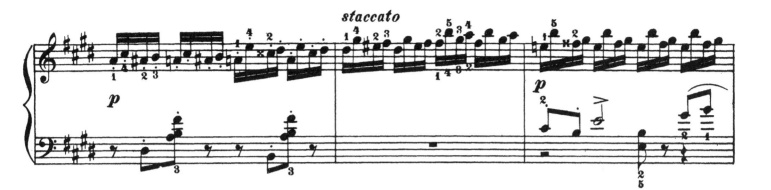

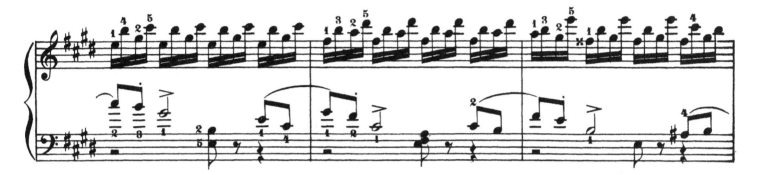

MORNING PRAYER

from *Album for the Young*

Pyotr Il'yich Tchaikovsky
Op. 39, No. 1

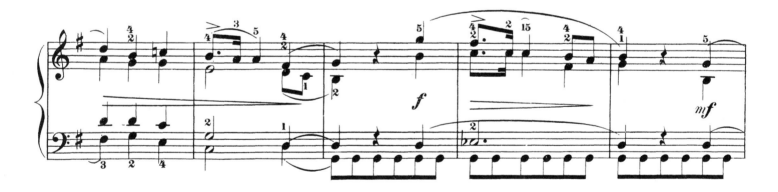